In the Backhoe's Shadow

In the Backhoe's Shadow

Poems

Thomas Alan Holmes

Iris Press
Oak Ridge, Tennessee

Cover Photo: Paul Gray

Author Photo: Michelle Joy Handler

Book Design: Robert B. Cumming, Jr.

Library of Congress Cataloging-in-Publication Data

Names: Holmes, Thomas Alan, author.
Title: In the backhoe's shadow : poems / Thomas Alan Holmes.
Description: Oak Ridge, Tennessee : Iris Press, [2022] | Summary: "In the
    backhoe's shadow, one takes a brief rest in the midst of
    responsibilities and needs, considering what comes next. In his debut
    poetry collection, In the Backhoe's Shadow, Thomas Alan Holmes offers a
    measured evaluation of a lost past, balancing the consequences of
    generational shift with expanded understanding of family, love, and
    place. At turns pastoral, lyrical, contemplative, descriptive, and,
    sometimes, playful, the collection explores how to sustain after years
    of separation the virtues of the stream, the pasture, and the hive"—
    Provided by publisher.
Identifiers: LCCN 2022023589 (print) | LCCN 2022023590 (ebook) | ISBN
    9781604542684 (paperback) | ISBN 9781604548211 (ebook)
Subjects: LCGFT: Poetry.
Classification: LCC PS3608.O49435623 I5 2022 (print) | LCC
    PS3608.O49435623 (ebook) | DDC 813/.6—dc23/eng/20220518
LC record available at https://lccn.loc.gov/2022023589
LC ebook record available at https://lccn.loc.gov/2022023590

Acknowledgments:

The author gratefully acknowledges the publications where poems in this collection first appeared, sometimes in slightly different forms:

Anthology of Appalachian Writers: "Over Cheeseburgers at the Cottage, Thomas Crofts and I Overhear a Valuable Lesson on Mortality from the Raconteur, an Esteemed Former Colleague"
Appalachian Heritage: "Molly in a Red Wig Plays a Fiddle"
Appalachian Journal: "Croquet" and "Secret Star"
Appalachian Places: "Knife" and "Pearl"
Avalon Literary Review: "Covenant"
Big Muddy: "Thomas Crofts and I Sing Tammy Wynette Songs in the Music Department Stairwell"
Cape Rock Journal: "'67 Bonneville, Goodbye"
Common Ground Review: "Because Cucumbers"
The Connecticut Review: "Mandolin"
Crannóg: "Thirst"
Drafthorse: "Mulberries"
The Examined Life: "Thomas Crofts and I Consider Haruspication and Routine Examinations of Middle-Aged Men"
The Florida Review: "Strength"
The Gulf Stream: Poems of the Gulf Coast: "Gulf Shores, 1968" and "Pascagoula"
The Howl: A Literary and Art Review: "Blind Cat"
Kentucky Writers: The Deus Loci and the Lyrical Landscape: "Lost Pasture"
Louisiana Literature: "Copperhead" and "Jones Valley"
Motif 2: Come What May: An Anthology of Writings about Chance: "Rolling Boil"
Motif 4: Seeking Its Own Level: An Anthology of Writings about Water: "Trencher"
Noctua Review: "Stray"
Now & Then: The Appalachian Magazine: "Good Dog"
The Pikeville Review: "Mekong"
Red Sky Journal: "Beekeeper"
The Southern Poetry Anthology, Volume III: Contemporary Appalachia: "Awning" and "Remember Roni Stoneman"
Steel Toe Review: "Caps" and "Drawer"
Still: The Journal: "Dowsing" and "Old 31"
Stoneboat: "Tissue"
Valparaiso Poetry Review: "Dish"

My wife, Barbara, and our children, Woody, Andy, and Maggie, have shown me a lot of affectionate patience and support as I have written these poems, and I am grateful for them. I appreciate that my parents, Earl Carlton and Mona Jane Holmes, assured my boyhood home was full of books and music.

I thank Roxanne Harde for proving to me that I should not let a worthwhile but stalled project lie fallow.

I thank Tess Lloyd and Marianne Worthington for introducing me to the community of creative writers in our region of Appalachia. I thank Crystal Wilkinson and William Wright for the encouragement they have given me, and I thank Charlotte Pence and Susan O'Dell Underwood for reviewing this manuscript and offering helpful different perspectives as I developed it. I thank Linda Parsons and Stellasue Lee for their good faith and their providing me a space to present my work.

I owe more to Darnell Arnoult and Denton Loving than I realize, and I am not the only person I know who can say that.

Finally, I am grateful for a fine circle of colleagues, Michael Cody, Thomas Crofts, Phyllis Thompson, Dan Westover, Catherine Pritchard Childress, and Jesse Graves, who have without fail encouraged me in my creative endeavors and continue to do so.

Contents

I.

Jones Valley

There was a walnut here;
wind broke it. A cedar thrives
now, offering meager shade
for survivors too past loss
to grieve. We count uncles
and aunts, those here, most at rest;
we stay long enough to watch
your cousins roll up plastic
rugs from around the grave's mouth.
You pull a rose from a spray
and toss it onto her casket.

From this hillside we see fields
fallow for years, overgrown,
pastures forced empty by drought,
winter feed costs, corporate
farms unable to recognize
any livestock dignity
respected by real farmers
who know a beast's potential
unpredictability
and stand wary, set to jump
out of the way, quick to grab
a blunt horn or a harness
or to strike hard and stand firm.

My family farmed here,
left here for Indiana,
returned here just as broke,
homesick, sick of Yankees,
sick of mockery from those
only a generation
more assimilated.

It was better to walk past
old home places lost to us,
unmade crops, mortgages,
so many sons gone to war,
still up north, not coming back,

having children who mock us
for being backward, Southern,
country, when we are cautious,
rooted, country without sneer,
without derision or shame.

I would like to go back
and give your newlywed
parents that hundred dollars
that would have saved that pasture.

I would like to join those men
waiting in the backhoe's shadow.
I can hear their radio
turned down in respect, of course,
but hinting of tackles
and first downs.

        I would like
to drive you to that spring
on our old home place, and squeeze
green peppermint leaves and drink
ice-cold water until my jaws
ache as we ache as my heart aches.

Matinee

By mid-July, hot patches on the pavement
would be soft enough so Lynn and I
could pry the bottle caps from tar
that edged the curb outside Mann's corner store.
The Martin Theatre held Wednesday morning
matinees, and eighteen Royal Crown caps
admitted both of us and Mom
to air-conditioning and movies in their second run:
Dean Jones in scratchy Disney frames,
or Elvis having trouble with another girl,
a color Stooges movie where they looked
too old and had a Curly that I didn't know.
If caps were upside down, they might
be Nehi, Coke, or Tab. We searched about
an hour; we could never bring ourselves
to ask for caps when big kids left the store
with sweaty cold drink bottles dripping wet,
and Mrs. Mann did not want us inside.
Two barefoot, buzzcut blonds, I see us hopping
step to step and hunting RC caps,
in hopes we'd tell Dad what we saw
and take his mind from truck repairs
and mortgages, the costs of life we couldn't see.

Copperhead

One weekend when Mom
drove out east to fetch my Dad
from Fort Benning, I stayed
the night with her parents,
Pawpaw and Mammaw. I was
their first grandson and didn't
yet know about the uncle
they had not mentioned to me,
lung cancer that would consume
my grandfather in eight years,
or that the Great Depression
still affected them even
in the early sixties.
I just knew that they watched
Bonanza on Sunday night,
and kept syrup every meal,
and Pawpaw drank his coffee
from his saucer, and their house
didn't have a bathroom.

Oh, they had running water.
I spent some steamy days
in and out of that kitchen
while Mammaw canned tomatoes
in everything from Mason
jars to old mayonnaise
jars, reusing lids older
than me, in and out to find
trails of moles in that grassless
yard just hardly cleared woods
for their new three-room
house, a great room combining
kitchen and living room,
their bedroom with wrought-iron
bedstead, a chifferobe, and no
closet, and a storage room
that would become a toilet
but then having only
a lidded pail, dead center

under a pullcord dangling
from an unshaded lightbulb.

Shame and modesty kept me
out of that room, mostly.

And Pawpaw, a carpenter,
had built a new pine outhouse
only a few yards away,
containing toilet paper
and old Sears catalogs,
depending on personal
preference, and I could not
bring myself to perch there,
but I could stand the smell
about long enough to pee
with someone outside waiting
to assure their town grandchild
would not fall in or get stuck.

I had heard their stories
and knew that moles meant snakes.
Uncle Ed, almost eighty,
when a boy about my age,
got rattlesnake bit and ran
(you were never supposed to run),
and Great-Granmaw grabbed a hen
and ripped its thigh off, pressing
its raw leg to Ed's bite
until chicken flesh turned all green
from absorbing poison,
Pawpaw had to feed Mom's dog
fresh lard for three days before
it could recover from getting
bitten on its face, and one fall
Mom herself had stepped just shy
of a rattler's head and stood
screaming as it coiled around
her ankles, unable

to bite or flee, whipping
its rattles and shaking them.
We knew snakes, we counted marks
and rattles, the Bible warned
us about them, and every
hoe and spade on Pawpaw's farm
had killed at least one or two.

I knew these things and snuck
outside by myself. I had
to go and thought it would be
better not to disturb them
after a long week of work
and a long, long day of church.
I could not wait to sit until
late Monday afternoon, when
I got home with Mom and Dad.

Once in that dim outhouse,
I could not see corners well,
and I could not smell that
cucumber copperhead smell.
Perched, though, I could see it,
as sunlight beneath the door
reached inside about a foot.
I stretched my legs straight out
and braced stiff-armed on either
side of the seat. I did not
yell, at first. I wanted to,
but I could not remember
if snakes reacted to noise;
a dog, I knew, would snap,
but snakes were tricky, evil,
just as likely to act calm
before biting as to give
a boy any warning. Its
head seemed to hover in place,
just above the plank floor,

and my arms were getting tired,
and the seat was just too big.

I do not think that I screamed,
but I yelled, hoping Hoss
and Little Joe weren't fighting,
because that was always
Pawpaw's favorite part,
the affection of those punches,
just rambunctious good fun
that Ben could stop with a word
and end any hard feelings
every bit as quick. I yelled,
and I heard the backdoor bang
against the wall and then
his heavy running steps.
He had a hoe in hand
and chopped fast. Snake parts wriggled
as he lifted me pants down
from my perch and stood me
in the yard. Mammaw scolded
us both, I remember,
and he cut me a look
that glowed after I tugged up
my pants and he put his hand
on my shoulder and led me
inside and waited while
I washed up and he listened
to my simple prayers and he
watched me climb on the pallet
next to the bed and told me
to go on to sleep and brushed
my forehead with the back
of his hand and walked into
the harping voice outside
the bedroom door. He was big
then and always will be.

Gulf Shores, 1968

At seven and nine, my brother and I
elbow prop, stomach down in the surf,
pink and brown from the sun, souvenir sailor caps
from the battleship moored in Mobile,

and our car is stuck. Dad digs in loose sand,
but the Pontiac's near bottomed out,
while our Mom keeps her vigil for riderless boards,
hint of undertow, and man-of-war.

Awning

Beneath a beauty parlor,
Cullman Awning Company,
my dad's own self-employment,
lay only small town blocks away
from our home, just far enough
to warm up his truck's engine.

A younger man, most evenings,
on worknights, after supper,
he parched peanuts, filling home
with rich smells of toasted shells;
earthy, red-skinned roasted peanuts
tasted good when dropped in Coke.

From corrugated metal
and aluminum square tubing,
he built made-to-order awnings
bearing fifty years of weather
all across north Alabama.
That bandsaw hurt his hearing
after years; after years
my teeth clamp on edge
as I think of shrieking metal
and imagine pampered
ladies seated under
Space Age plastic dryer
domes in preparation
for their Pentecostal
towering hair. AquaNet
never filtered down enough
to contend with musty
metallic tang and sawdust
I swept up those special days
that I could go with Dad to work.

When his time comes, and by God
I am not prepared for it,
I would shell him like peanuts
and strip his old man hull

to free his blond-haired, red-armed
self whose blue eyes wink at me
beneath angel floss white brows.

Caps

What year was it, Dad, that you
and Johnny Horton, digging
ditches for rural water,
hit the blasting caps
with your trencher? I can see
you in your truck, with Johnny
curled in the passenger seat,
and how you still looked dazed
once you screeched into the driveway
and both climbed into the car
as you told me to tell Mom
you were driving down
to Birmingham, forty-five
miles away. Although you
got back soon, I didn't
know for years that you had felt
the sweat pour down your face
and didn't touch your scalp
for fear that you had burst
your skull. You'd kept us from
the car, believing we would see
your brain exposed to God knows
what. It's been a great, long time
since then, and Johnny died
from cigarettes, and you've
got grit in your eyes like
from a shotgun blast, but you've
outlasted melanoma,
spinal surgery, and flu
a bunch of times. I know
I'll never see you in an
ambulance, I never will,
but tomorrow I'd buy us
a trencher, load your truck
with PVC pipe, and dig
new waterlines up 31
from Hurricane Creek
to Mallard Point.

Trencher

Dad drove up with a trencher hitched
behind a Ford truck green as June,
a brand-new orange Ditch Witch, squat
and mildly dangerous both ends.
The county wanted water lines
to tap the city reservoir,
and we dug through packed dirt so parched
it fell into the trench, through clay
so red and sticky viscous we
took sticks to pry clean trencher teeth.
In churchyard property, I swirled
the dope to meld pipe fittings, nose
too used to cyarn to care. We'd cut
through asphalt, gravel coarse as cuss,
break digging chains with brick-sized links
and bend pins bootheel thick. And there
was shit: one pigsty wallow, muck
wheel high, mid-thigh, I lost a boot
and doubted reaching for it, squeezed
it on, and flinched. The meter tapped,
we settled up; that first cold gush
of wet washed off the slop and left
us dripping on the leatherette
upholstery and rubber mats.
Hot August whipping, glass rolled down,
we hightailed home to load the pipe,
eat up, and scrub the done day gone.

Dowsing

Wrist up, you hold a prong in each
inverted hand, thumbs out, and point
the joined limb skyward, forearms raised,
your knuckles pressed to sternum. Lift
your shoulders. Back and head erect,
you step toe-heel toe-heel and wait
until the water underground
tugs downward at the single tip,
your body a mere conduit
between the thirsty wood and water; they
will pull; the water draws the stick;
the stick will force your forearms down.
You kick a bootheel divot; dig.

Remember Roni Stoneman

Do you remember Roni Stoneman
on our old black-and-white Zenith,
picking banjo every Saturday
just after Dad got home from work
and you were broiling club steaks
that our butcher, Mr. Dutton,
sawed from short loin just that morning?
In the kitchen, dicing peppers,
some Vidalias, some tomatoes
for a salad, Old Dutch dressing
sweetly mixed up with my ketchup
on fake Dresden-themed blue dishes
that we bought from Sears and Roebuck
that first summer we cleared money,
that first summer I was mowing
so that Dad no longer had to,
before dates took weekend evenings,
graduation took me further,
then my job so many miles away
from syndicated bluegrass
and fresh-showered weekend evenings
when a day of rest starts early
and a blessing is a table
with someone at every chair?

Oh, Mama, Roni Stoneman,
wearing pigtails, a grown woman,
slightly wall-eyed, slightly buck-toothed,
and buckdancing between breakdowns—
was it meant to be a costume,
was it Sadie Hawkins cuteness,
like some Minnie Pearl theatrics
before *Hee Haw* turned her ugly,
and she put her banjo down?

I remember Roni Stoneman,
motor oil and sweat-through workshirts,
Porter Wagoner and Dolly
hawking dishcloths in detergent,

sharp-scent dandelion, horsenettle,
Martha White self-rising flour,
Flatt and Scruggs, and Wally Fowler,
Prell and Go-Jo, Zest and Lifebuoy,
pressure cookers, canned tomatoes,
gasoline and garden hoses,
six-day workweeks as we knew them,
spending Saturdays in summer
finding rest about sundown.

Cursive

My mother's teachers taught her penmanship,
the perfect loops, like Disney title cards
and bowling alley signs, elliptical
and proper for a virginal
young Baptist in the Eisenhower years.

Money came here last,
a party line at Mammaw's house,
electric pumps for sulfurous well water,
teen idol pop for privileged girls in town,
the county seat a half an hour lost,
the brand-new interstate a farm road hour's drive away.

Today her briefest notes
still signify a scrubbed-clean girl
in handsewn poplin dress
and rhinestone-studded cateyes.

Minibike

We had a minibike,
a Briggs and Stratton
lawnmower engine
mounted in red steel.

We wore a dirt track
through some tight spaces,
just missing tool sheds
and some pecan trees.

Mom had a rosebush
close to the clothesline.
Lynn rode right through it—
not quite right through it

We heard him yelling,
stuck in the middle,
pulled rose stems from him,
laughing and sorry.

In a few minutes,
he had stopped bleeding.
He went back riding.
It was his turn.

Croquet

Outside our mother's kitchen window, yard
like Carolina flat like Tuscaloosa soil
of sand and gravel, grassy, clover covered, Lynn
and I had grown beyond the wooden pegs
and mallets, wickets made of wire
like white coat hangers, and were digging holes
and tunnels for the painted wooden balls.
We'd spent the summer banging ankles, every mallet miss
of croquet balls we held in place barefooted, shots
so far beyond our little lot they'd sometimes scoot
across First Street into the Germans' yard.
June hot as August, we would walk
three blocks to fish bare forearm deep
inside the icy cooler at White's Grocery,
drinking there to save deposit, finding softened tar
along the street and leaving whorls from naked heels;
we walked to Nesmith Pool in bathing suits
and towels fresh from the clothesline,
our admission quarters in our pockets, leave
brown footprints wet, evaporating, blurred
with splashes from tight cannonballs,
bad somersaults, sore belly flops that shamed
the dizzy boys who clambered to pool's edge
and climbed the ladder where the diving board
rebounded from a bounce of fiberglass
and metal, thunder summer, Cullman, boys,
butch haircuts, brown, in Alabama, home.

II.

Mandolin

Away with the noise of your songs! I will not listen to the music of your harps.
—Amos 5:23

Too big a man to hold
a plaything, husband, set
it down, your mandolin.

There lie no mines for miles
around. You've always farmed
or found some joinery.

There's no black lung, no shafts
like graves; we've sun and rain,
a roof for night's relief.

God would not hear from strings—
the Scripture tells us so,
no hymns from mandolins,

such meager instruments
for praising Him. The Lord
told Amos set them down.

No lover lost, no one
forsaking you, no pain
from broken hearts, none gone,

we have our lives. To hold
a baby, husband, think
of it, to have a son.

To ramble on the road
is daydream, husband, meant
for boys who have no home.

To sing of taking off
and straying from your roots
might count among your sins.

We have a life to piece
together, husband. Set
it down, your mandolin.

Strength

Pa knows that my brother is a stronger man
than I am. He always takes Print to town
to load the pickup. He never takes me.
I'll stand waiting to lift something heavy,
and he'll always go to Print for help.
I love Pa, and Ma, too, and I don't mind
helping her with the woman's work.
I'll set the table or hang out the clothes for her,
but I want a man's work.
I want Pa to see how I can whip
every boy in my school, just about,
except Print.
Even last year, when I heard
him laugh as I walked from the clothesline,
I couldn't whip him. I dropped the basket
and jumped toward him,
and when he picked up some kindling,
I grabbed a hatchet, ready to swing.
"You won't hit me," he said.
I stared at him and said that I would.
He threw down the kindling, spat, and walked
to the chopping block. "Cut me," he said,
laying his right hand palm up, watching me sweat.
He watched me raise the hatchet higher;
he watched my eyes
while I cut off his second and third fingers.
I got the basin and the kerosene to stop the bleeding,
and I bandaged him.

Mekong

I.

It sounded like a Southern place,
a delta, where my brother went
to be a sailor. He, up in these hills,
had joined the Navy, who
had never seen the ocean, raised
two counties from a river, just
the creeks and shallow ponds
to water stock and baptize old-
clothes frightened Christians strong in Christ
but wary of the preacher's tired old arms.
"At arms" is what he called our boys
at war, and three from our own church,
at war with Communists who beat the French.
My dad had fought to save those French
and kept his medals in a box. At school,
the science teacher had a folded sleeve
to cover what he'd lost. Mom kept the news
turned off at supper time but turned it on
once she sent me to bed. My dad
said nothing at commercial breaks.

II.

What did I know of soldiers then
but Gomer Pyle, who never got deployed,
and Sad Sack in my comic books, always
at camp and stoic as Lakota chiefs
on *Gunsmoke*, where the only war was over, fought
by blues and grays who, nobly, kept their peace.
So many comic books with super men,
all fighting stupid criminals whose plans
would fall apart, who'd wait one at a time
to fight the hero, wearing costumes anyone
would spot from blocks away. I bought them wrapped
in cellophane, their covers gone, "stripped" books
I didn't know our grocer sold against

the law, but they were cheap. I never knew
what comic of the bundled three I'd find
stuck in between, but I would read them all.
And then, one day I saw the ad, a small
gray submarine with kids inside. I saved
for weeks and dreamed of taking off to find
the Mekong Delta, find my brother, fight
a mission, bring him home to Mom and Dad.
My submarine—*The Can of Steel*—would find
its way to Panama, cut through, and head
out west across the ocean. I would drag
it to the pond and learn to navigate,
to dive and fire, to rescue, and come home.

III.

He's still alive, my brother, older than
my father was back then. His body worked
against itself in time; presciptions dull
his short-term memory. He tells the same
old stories every time I see him, like
dementia patients, but he gets names right,
and soon he'll need a chair. He wasn't shot
or captured, and he seemed like his old self
when he got back. He married only once.
He preaches to an earnest group of folks
and votes Republican; he always has.

IV.

I spent my birthday money. In five weeks
it came, all bundled up with plastic straps,
a corrugated cardboard submarine
all folded up in pieces, portholes black
and smudged and printed on the sides, the hatch
a flap behind the hatbox turret. I
fit tabs and slots in tears, too big a boy
to fit inside. I creased it, split some seams,

and left it in the yard out by the porch.
The morning dew next day had curled each edge.
I burned it in the trash pile, after school.

V.

In "Basic Fitness," ROTC, out
and running mornings before dawn, I learned
how many students signed in hopes they'd earn
commissions just to cover college costs, aware
that war could take them overseas but now
concerned that they could run a two-mile course
in less than eighteen minutes, pass the tests
for calisthenics, keep their grades in line.
I took the class three times, assured how much
I liked my classmates, how bravado turned
to confidence, how fun they were, how once
they saw that I was there to learn with them
they trusted me to push myself until
I couldn't stand and laughed when at the pool
I, too, would climb the platform, rifle clutched
in both my hands, blindfolded, and would leap
into the deep end, laughing loud with me,
a prof old as their dads, who had enough
good faith in them to take that leap. I watched
some earn their bars and graduate; I think
of them, Iraq, Afghanistan, deployed;
I see us: past the soccer fields, wet grass
in late October, counting sit-ups, breath
just visible, and, grunting, thistle stung,
and aching, we could smell just past the rise
the Daylight Doughnuts shop and curse DIs
for pushing us towards the paths we chose.

Blind Cat

By eleven, my vision
had blurred—even my mother
passed in scudding grays, and days
vanished when sunlight's red traces
pulsed inside my eyelids—
no difference, open, closed,
head up or down, only heat
and air, clothesline smell, packed earth,
locust crack in thunderstorms,
and pressure cooker scuffle.

I climbed trees outside our yard,
ran across pastures, and dunked
cousins in our Pappaw's pond.
I dreaded bedtime most nights,
just yearning to stay outside,
mosquito bait, not to lie
sweating and waiting for sleep,
open-window radio,
moist night breath and curled grass, slight
weight of sky on my shoulders,
my bare feet springing from earth
with a tire swing, truckbed rush.

Our old tabby queen's litter
of five turned out a blind runt.
We didn't know for weeks,
until she weaned them and it
began its pitiful mewling.

We did not name that kitten.
Ma fed it to quiet it,
but I never petted it.
I was not sorry when Pa
took its skin and stretched it.
My new banjo's head felt smooth,
smoother than my sister's face,
salted wash of ice cream churn,
dandelion puff, prayer whisper.

I fretted with strings and keys;
at last music came through me,
until I felt air and curled grass,
seeing sunlit silhouettes
of children traipsing down
windsnap corridors of white,
clothespinned, lifeworn bedsheets.

Dish

Her fluted serving bowl,
the only thing I kept, is green,
emblazoned with a rooster
in the bottom, its comb
three crosshatched teardrops, like
its single teardrop wattle.
Its breast bears arrows, curling
towards its tail. Whenever
she boiled cubed potatoes
buttery and salty, she
would serve them in this dish,
the best of her depression
service. Yellow melted beads
of butter bobbed in boiling
water, coalescing
as the dish cooled and emptied,
leaving the rooster beneath
a shallow, golden lens.

Covenant

My girls were easier,
some unexpected blood
and feeling sick, and sin
so firmly lodged in flesh,
with Hattie Jean especially
in shame and hiding how
she washed her bloody drawers.
No one can keep a secret
from a wife who washes clothes.

But that boy, Welton, slathered
up in sticky grease well past
his elbows, scorch of motor oil
and gasoline's sharp smell,
and outside, paying me no mind
no matter how I pecked
the kitchen window, called to him,
yelled at him through the screen door—
he would not turn to me,
waist deep beneath the hood,
a young man eying life,
already driving backroads
and him only turned thirteen.
He looked sidewise when fetching
mail, especially
those catalogs, creased pages
showing where he peeked
at women's undergarments.
The girls were bleeding by
thirteen, and blood kept them
from sin. His clothes just reeked
of man, not child's sweet sweat,
but hard and rank and grown.

So when the minister began
to speak of covenants with God,
I found my answer, God,
who struck at Moses, God
who killed the first born, God,

whose Son cleans us with blood,
redeeming sin with blood, as I
have done, could do for mine.
But like a man, my husband Earl
paid me no mind. "Carlie, we can't,"
he said, "It's too late now.
He's almost grown. We couldn't then.
Our crops were poor that year."
"The Lord provided, nonetheless,"
I answered, staring straight, but he
kept on, "Old Granny Guthrie
wouldn't, and her vision had
gone bad. A newborn doesn't know,
but Welton would. He isn't ours
to do with as we will."
"Of course he is not ours,"
I said, "but loaned from God
for us to make prepared
for Him to judge at this world's end."
My vow to be his helpmate means
I guide him time to time.

And so I prayed and asked
our minister, the meekest man
and kind, if we should turn
to Exodus. And so we prayed
and so he preached four weekends straight
of sin and flesh and God's complete
and perfect need that we perform
His will, delivering to Him
ourselves as instruments
as He justly requires.
That boy, who loved Earl more
than anyone else could,
somehow, somehow came to believe
that God would strike his father down
should Welton not submit. Praise Christ
for guiding me to Zipporah!

The Morgan County Health
Department doctor let
Earl stay beside the boy but kept
me out; still, God was there
to lay hands on their souls.
From that day on, they always
spoke with quiet words
when they should speak to me.
The scarring meant more surgery,
and Welton took to woods
and fields; he hardly eyed
the road 'til war broke out.

When I birthed two more sons,
Earl had them circumcised
before we brought them home.

Lost Pasture

The last time I stood in the pasture, clover bunched
to my midshin, and bees were busy, petaled puffs
of clover bobbing when they clung to blossoms round
as life is round, the egg, the eye, the open mouth,
and I was calm among the bees, the clover bunched
midshin, and I could smell the beeves across the stream
that curled from underneath the hill, a cave as low
as half a room, the water cold enough to blue
my feet in minutes 'til I climbed to find relief
among the sunny bee-filled clover, lowing beeves
as drowsy as the bobbing clover blossoms clung
to almost lovingly by bees at work as I
would stand to watch the sky vault blue, the subtle drone,
the lowing, bees on clover blossoms bobbing low
as soft as warming earth I pressed between my toes
as they dug in like tendriled, hungry roots to home.

Beekeeper

Veiled and gentle he
deliberate and slow would lift
the honeyed inner frame and rob.
I've watched him with a fingertip
nudge setting bees from his bare wrist
with no more force than inheld breath
when turning keys, relieved at home.

Old and patient he
considerate would dote on boys
he never saw mature to men.
I, once a child who grew to learn
of blessed and meek poverty
and hungry stoicism, heard
him tell his neighbor bees our lives.

Two summers gone I halted
when a worker lit inside
the right lens of my glasses.
I'd learned to raise my steady hand
to my left temple, lift
my glasses from my face,
and let the bee fly free.

It seemed but within weeks,
a queen had found a hollow
a few paces from our path
up to our porch, the swarm
for three days pulsing
as my young ones veered, in fear
they might be stung. I strode
up to the trunk and jumped
and yelled and whooped so they
would laugh and understand
a queen will mind her work
with life's commotion all around.

This morning, though, was cold
and wet as we could not

expect, and still I hoped
the sky when I got home
November afternoon
would clear enough to stir
the hive, that I might see
just one of those who hovered
days ago, but none was there,
all clustered deep inside
the well of that old tree.

And so my son, turned back
to watch the path up to our porch,
has seen me stand and call
the huddled hive in hollow
sassafras, "Our friend has died.
Oh, our friend has died. Oh,
our friend has died."

Thirst

Deep clover of our fenced-in pasture
offered handholds as we braced
ourselves beside an icy spring
that whispered from the hill's low cave.
There on the bank, where nettle met
green rushes, we would kneel
and dip our picnic cups for drinks
so cold they chilled like nascent ice,
the spring so clear we saw round pebbles
we could grasp if we would dare
to lean and stretch and numb
our reach up past our wrists.

Away, I never drink without
a thirsty heart.

III.

'67 Bonneville, Goodbye

So much metal, so much engine, so much chrome,
so out of place among the Reagan-era undergraduates' new BMWs,
your avian front bumper,
your turquoise leatherette upholstery that matched the paint,
your hardtop watersanded for a brand-new pearl-white roof,
your growling carburetor, raw, four-barrel, raw,
in parking lots, on errands, stuck
in traffic, still I think of you.

My uncle bought you back
for restoration, then, consumed
with fuel consumption, stripped
you down, removed your trim
and fender skirts, free-wheeled
you down steep grades, and locked
your thirsty tank.

And now, you're gone, most likely crushed
to cube and melted down,
but I would like to think
you're in a barn somewhere,
beneath a tarp, and some ol' boy
is scavenging the salvage yards
of backroad Alabama
for a blue acrylic steering wheel,
a deep-throat carburetor, fender skirts,
and trim.

Drawer

With every move we never
sort, so as we settled in
and you began to fill
the empty dresser drawers,
you stopped and held it out,
your red slip with the side split.

I smile and do not say
how we'd left a reception
in Morgan Hall, stopped to pick
some papers from my office,
and got tangled, how your
boy-cut lacy panties
weren't the same red as your slip,
how your black hose had a hole
at the heel. I remember
the turquoise nightie you wore
only once, coming downstairs
when we'd just moved into our
Tuscaloosa townhouse,
but then, those years before kids,
you'd come to bed in my blue
faded Jackson Browne t-shirt.

I wrote you this love poem,
the only way you'll know
what I've kept secreted
in the back of my sock drawer.

Stray

Lying in our marriage bed,
lying side by side,
I listen to the house and to your breath.

We lay like this for years,
apartments, rented houses, mortgage.

The Tuscaloosa townhouse, best
when, thunderstorming, we could open
windows, feeling ozone
in the wet air.

Doubt scratched the door.

On top of the bedspread, sweaty, tired,
reluctant to get dressed, we lay;

Doubt nosed and whined at us;
it wanted fed and walked.

That past winter, Doubt had circled
all the books piled in the living room,
sniffing what I studied
for preliminary tests;
it would have gnawed a keyboard.

We couldn't break Doubt from gnawing.

As I walked between buildings,
tired from hours of mass grading,
eyes as dry as empty ballpoints,
Doubt would pad along the sidewalk,
lick my fingers, and fall back.

Doubt bears its teeth at smiles;
it growls at chuckles,
barks at laughs.

At times, Doubt lies on its back
and wants a belly rub;
I give it heartworm tablets,
treat for fleas, watch for ticks.

It snaps at our own children
after a long day.
I yank it by the collar
when it seems about to bite.

And animal control
won't haul it off; I lack the heart
to put it down myself.
If I drove it to the country
and set it loose,
it would come back again.

Doubt trailed us north from Knoxville,
making it past Pigeon Forge,
and kept our northbound track, with Asheville
just a veer to the right; we slept one night
but heard it
baying as if we were treed.

I don't know anyone who'd like to take
this dog.

One time, I played ball with
puppy Doubt;
it knew I held it in my hidden hand.
It did not turn its head, its eyes
so fixed, I saw no whites,
just coffee color ringing black.

Full grown, Doubt stands pants pocket level.

I wanted a border collie—they're so smart—
to help run the place.

Doubt has no pedigree—
it's from so many breeds—
and I've not fixed it yet,
and it might get out.

And Doubt is ravenous.
I don't intend to feed it, but I do,
when I'm hungry.

Doubt circles us
when we're at the table.
Doubt knows we will not feed it,
but it snaps up what we drop.

And sometimes, when it storms,
I stand on the porch
to love the thunder, the lightning, you.
Then, I hear padfall, all through the house,
heavy. I call Doubt, calm Doubt
just enough, I hope, to stop
its leaping through screened windows
or the safety glass storm door.

Tissue

Your very first afternoon,
the neonatal unit,
and Mom recovering doors down,
I stood in stiff blue scrubs
and heard a nurse insist
your Mammaw and Pawpaw Holmes,
from seven hours on the road,
wear disposable coveralls
yellow as a kitchen sponge,
before she'd bring you, when
I'd have grabbed a blanket,
taken you outside, and met
them in the parking lot.
They felt, the coveralls,
a bit like fibrous filters
on the heat pump intake
register, but folded
like the paper towels
in cardboard dispensers
above supermarket
meat counters. I hadn't
seen my Dad move that fast
since years before, while we
repaired a wind-ripped school,
and a blast blew over me
a dilapidated
section of aluminum
walkway cover. We raced home;
he'd been sure I'd been cut
or crushed, but I was safe
as ever we can be safe.
And to meet you, he threw on
that papery suit, faster
than Mammaw, to get you
in his hands, the first day
that you were one of the kids
to guard against an empty
gut, a vacant heart, a dull
mind, an unexpected gust.

Batter Head

The batter head, the rim, the sticks themselves,
sometimes no sticks at all but only hands
that you might cup or arch or flex to coax
a sound. Your mallets make the rosewood bars
respond to touch for tones no string or horn
can match. You'll pound on pottery. I've heard
you join with others in time signatures
so far beyond my customary count
I felt as if I'd stumble when you stopped.
I've seen you roll three mallets in each hand.
Sometimes you'll sit and set your limbs in their
own time, direct yourself in all directions—how
we'd sit at meals and you without a thought
would tap your fingers on the table, lift
your heel as if a pedal rested there,
and thud the floor! I learned the batter head
receives the strike, the other head responds
in resonance to make the note complete.
Whenever you sit still, I count the time
and register what rhythm might erupt.

Pearl

I've seen you swap it up, the cymbal crash,
the challenge to play keyboard, march the miles,
emote on cue for football stadiums,
encouraging your bandmates, pushing carts
and loading trucks, halftime percussion pit.

I've known you sit for hours drawing hands.

You could have drifted as another flute
among the flutes, except, not you, you took
bassoon, so tall with its own voice, distinct
but fitting in, but filling in, once missed,
a needed complement to melody,
foundation, contrapuntal, subtle, strong.

I think you learned before your brothers did
how much it hurts to care. You never stop,
all too aware that open arms leave hearts
without defense, so what is fierce and brave
can bear the hopeful child their whole life long.

Good Dog

These seven years, you taught
our little girl to watch
a water bowl and keep
it full, to listen for
a whine beside a door,
to cup a face with love
without a word. Good dog.

You helped our house feel full.
What if you sat too close
or licked more than we liked?
You wagged from shoulder back
and nosed our palms and watched
us live, reminding us
routine is blessed. Good dog.

Tonight, as our house sets,
I yearn to hear your claws
click down the hall and wait
for you to nose each door
ajar. Your bowl is dry,
but that end of the couch
is still your place. Good dog.

Knife

I bought bone-handled stockman Case, a green
dye in the bone I hadn't seen. I knew
it wouldn't be for show; he'd put it through
rough work, to pry a rusted-shut machine,
to slice an apple swiped on pants to clean,
to strip a wire, to shape the tire-patch goo
and striate rubber, too, and twist a screw
when thumbnails wouldn't do. It could have been
a Sunday knife, a precious thing, but he
knew what a knife was for and showed his pride
by making it do everything. Why be
reluctant? Take it. Let it slip inside
my pocket with his years' utility
kept folded in it ever since he's died.

Secret Star

As I was nine and innocent in my father's car,
lying face up in the back floorboard, watching the night sky
on a Christmas Eve, alert to see
a special light as I still believed
in that good holiday
and saw a steady white that did not blink I took for that star,
ignorant of astronomy, that every star would blink,
and likely saw Venus, white,
clear, and high in hard, cold December,

face up in that Pontiac, riding the two-lane highway
between country grandparents that Christmas Eve and our home
where I must fall asleep to welcome
good Santa Claus, I still believed
in him even at nine, innocent
of the story's effect on a child without neighboring kids
who could teach him some truths about fantasies, legends
intended as parable
blended in childish self-interest,

innocent yet suspecting the red steady light I saw
moving between our slow, highway-bound Pontiac driven
with care by my father, who prided
himself with his skills at the wheel
I could feel through the floorboard, face up,
smoothest movement, smooth gliding of tires over smooth pebbled
    pavement,
the star fixed in place, if in truth it was some star at all,
the red light's steady arcing
as if blinking pace with our trip home,

and my mother so happy we were all four together,
my brother asleep in the backseat unable to lie
steady rocking while riding awake
and her lilting soft talking to Dad
in the secret voice parents must use
to assure listening children who don't catch the words all is well
and as certain and steady as stars in the firmament

and faith she embraced, her heart
full of her love for us all riding

slow towards town, barely then claimed a city that would fill
with the franchises so that old stores named for our neighbors
would close on the main streets, offices
taking their places near the courthouse
where folks get their licenses, justice
now processed to maximize fines that can finance the gears
and careers of aspiring old money to win office,
directing the hard-working lives
of the modestly hopeful in love

with their families, taking them home from a brief visit
time could permit in the rush for what change I risked seeing
if I moved my gaze from that white star
that may not have been a star at all
to focus on that moving red light
that I believed could have been Santa Claus' sleigh in that clear night
racing so slowly, pacing us maybe, me safe in back,
my feeling the road rolling,
I was looking and lying in joy.

IV.

Thomas Crofts and I Deliberately Walk off the Job and Desecrate the Eastman Drive Starbucks by Smoking Camels in the Parking Lot

Sweet Christ, and it a Wednesday, we
had had enough and left the campus just
before the midday class began and ran
out to the parking lot where I had parked
a pick-up truck I'd bought downstate.
It was a Chevy older than my boys,
and it was rusted just a little on the wheel well. Damn!
It drove like new. We blew through two
stuck red lights, turning tight onto the interstate,
and rolled on 26 on out of town.
My truck still had an 8-track player, and
the tape was Willie Nelson, some live thing
with songs so long the tape jumped tracks
in some, but we were hollering, the windows down.
And I hate driving on the interstate.
You can't see anything but what's away,
the close stuff rushing past and blurred,
while two-lanes take your time and some ol' gal
who doesn't mind a man's appreciation waves
and poses just a little bit and smiles
in her surprise, but we were on the interstate
and rolling hell for leather, an expression I
once heard in an old movie with Lee Marvin, who
was fighting Nazis. "What about Lee Marvin?" I
asked Thomas Crofts, medievalist
and follower of history, a drummer
(that's a double whammy, by the way;
medievalists are idiosyncratic;
drummers follow their own beats).
"Just palimony, tough guy, Kid Shelleen
is all you need to know." As "Whiskey River" blent
into a gospel song at last, we then at last
decided corporation coffee would be fine
but couldn't smoke inside although I spoke
to the barista in *Hochdeutsch*
because, clairvoyant, I could tell
she missed her boyfriend's tongue.

Her manager, a shaved-pate man
who took up two whole tables with his books
and his computer and a replica
of some cult tv prop, decided I
should leave the premises. The cups too full
to drink and drive, we sat, Thomas and I,
to smoke some Camels in the parking lot.
We saw the fleshy apparition known
as Dancing Steve back in our town,
but here he had his hair tucked up
into a British driving cap and wore
some type of outfit I'd expect
Olivier to wear just like a spy.
We offered him a smoke, but when
he smiled we saw a whole lot more
than we intended to and rolled
our windows up. I cranked
the truck. It lurched and spilled
the cups, and off we went back south
to Johnson City. Thomas watched behind
as if he thought that Steve would chase
us down, but I was eying him
myself in my rearview. And we
took 36 on back and headed to the house,
convinced we'd see another Steve
at every intersection. Ghosts
are rooted to a place, and roads
are just one skinny place from here to there.

Thomas Crofts Has a Computer Problem, and I Start a Fire in His Office

When I was passing through the second floor,
Herr Doktor Thomas Crofts, medievalist,
delayed me with a question. "Why?"
he asked, and I, due stumped, decided we
should sit. I offered to step up to my
drear cell and grab my instrument
of solace, mandolin, while he could
noodle through a banjo tune when all
at once the power grid shut down,
and then the students all began
to act as if they'd never seen the dark.
I nearly shouted to them there
were windows in the classrooms, but in such
a situation, hope is lost. Then Thomas said,
"Let's lead benighted souls into the light."
He grabbed a student newspaper from off
his desk and rolled it pretty tight. I lit
it up, completely unaware
of Big Mac coupons, flammable
as gas, in my new torch. We smoked
six ceiling tiles in just an instant,
dropped the fire into a rubbish can,
and nudged it to the hall. The students ranged
around the fire like Christmas vagrants stuck
in Bristol for the holiday, afraid
to cross state lines. And I began
to sing beneath my breath of Molly Bán,
and Thomas got his banjo, and the hall
soon filled with senior faculty
who kept their flasks stuck in their desks.
"Oh, strange new world!" one of them said
and kissed my forehead hard.

Thomas Crofts, Jesse Graves, and I Witness a Death on the State of Franklin and Consider to What Degree We Have Been Diminished

The VA ducks who swim in ponds at Mountain Home
and often in the gully running east
to downtown Johnson City sometimes waddle out
into the road, and Thomas Crofts, medievalist,
and Jesse Graves and I were coming back
from eating German food downtown for May
Oktoberfest; the beer was crisp and cold,
the sauerbraten salty good, the schnitzel hot.
Before we'd reached our cruising speed,
with Jesse at the wheel and Thomas shotgun set,
I saw a primered Datsun zag around the skating rink
across from seed and feed, and, hooking left,
plow over a white duck. Its carcass lay
between white stripes. One of us muttered, "Damn!"
And then, as Neko Case began to sing
of heartbreak in a minor key, and I
began to wonder just how long the duck
would lie there in the road, a tree
branch blew athwart our windshield, rolled
across the roof, and fell into the path
of squad cars in formation in our wake.
"Our lunch has been of doubts,
uncertainties, and mysteries," said Jesse, hands
at ten and four, and Thomas smiled in half,
the lip curl on one side, and my tongue probed
a tiny bit of parsley at the corner of my mouth.

Thomas Crofts and I Consider Haruspication and Routine Examinations of Middle-Aged Men

Outside the English building, near the street,
I hold the map to my most inner self,
the pink and rounded corridor of flesh,
provided me when I awoke from dark
in digital, 600 dpi, my name
in bold across the top, results of tests,
the endoscopic plumber's snake they probed
down my esophagus, to foretell all.
My printout prophecy provided me
and Thomas Crofts, medievalist, the chance
and welcome opportunity to mourn
the mystery of life, now mapped the way
an unmanned Google car can plot a town.
I told him how the sweatbee sting, a vein
on my right hand, felt nothing like the bland
green plastic guide they had me bite down on
so that the camera probe would never touch
my teeth, my swollen, bitten lips, my fog
and doubt of what I might have said as I
awoke from anesthetic sleep. "And yet,"
he said, "far more routine and comic goes
the colonoscopy, in through the out,
as Led Zep punned, another orifice,
another oracle, to the same end,
to read our guts and tell us times to come."

Those "times to come"—before us stand in scrubs
of rainbow hue to designate the role
of each a surgeon's staff encircling one
who lies beneath an arc of burning white,
his abdomen split open to reveal
the sum of what has been and what's to come.
The surgeon speaks, "Let's have a poke around.
He has a chance at twenty years, but see
his gut distended, tears in tissue here,
the liver knobbiness—just close him up."
Supine, the patient turns to smile at us,

to gesture Blue Cross has OK'd our turn,
extended palm of state-insured in full.

I smirked to mask my gasp of churning guts,
reminded of a vivisected frog
my fourth-grade teacher, Mrs. Freeman, flayed
in front of us, its spinal cord in two
from her deft ice pick plunge. Her thumb was black
from silver nitrate. She had stopped me once
when I was wiping off electrolyte
from naked wires my partner had plugged in.

"I guess nobody told you," Thomas said,
"why is it men die early? 'Cause we can!"
I heard it echo from the science hall.
Then I fell hoarse from laughing, flecks of blood
sprayed on my wrist, and I took off alive,
relieved to have a rank companion free
to chide me, send me home to feed my kids,
to fall asleep turned on my side to grasp
my sweet one's hip, behind me the machine
that forces breath down through me as I sleep.

Thomas Crofts and I Break the Bounds of Earth; April, Late Cold and Wet

Bareheaded I, in denim trucker's jacket, black,
accompanied in earthy houndstooth overcoat
and baseball cap marked "Trinity"
friend Thomas Crofts, medievalist,
and, stepping from an alcove, found
a puddle two feet wide that we
both leapt across. We did not leap
like stags. We did not leap like flame.
We leapt like men, in asynchronous leap,
no grace, but purpose, landing flat
on sure-placed feet. Beyond us lay
wet pavement and dark skies,
yet in our leap we were between them both.

Thomas Crofts and I Sing Tammy Wynette Songs in the Music Department Stairwell

Intending to liberate
a vintage bassoon, Thomas
Crofts, medievalist, and I
climbed the clangy metal stairs
in the due northwest stairwell
of the Music Department.
"Just where," asked Thomas, "will we
find this seasoned instrument?"
"Just follow the stairway," I said,
noting the acoustics of blocks
and steel. Thomas noticed, too:
"To these arms of mine," he sang,
"You'll find me waiting here," pause,
"in apartment number nine."
Our next impromptu tribute
to Tammy Wynette, the queen
of heartbreak, was just starting,
and I, saving the duets
for later, began, "Your Good
Girl's Gonna Go Bad," answered
by his "I Don't Wanna Play
House." By now, the big jazz guy,
six eight and three hundred plus,
was breathing hard two landings
down, and we approached super
hits, linking "Stand by Your Man,"
"D-I-V-O-R-C-E,"
and, at long last, "Golden Ring,"
with Thomas singing as George,
usually the best song
for a finale, but jazz
guy wanted answers right then.
"What's going on, guys?" he asked,
and Thomas said, "We're stealing
a bassoon." And then we did.

Spontaneous Generation on the Watauga

For four nights running he slipped
from their bed, his wife asleep
as he opened the glass door
to their back deck, took the stoop
to the white clover-lined path
to their dock, glazed silver blue
by a gibbous moon. He stood
and gazed to the other shore
and opened his fly to piss.
The whispering Watauga
took in his halting relief
as it flowed to the Holston.
At once a great blue heron
rose from between the pilings,
unfolding itself, rising
into the air, its scrolled neck
ess-like before sharp angles
silver-blue in pure moonlight
like the clover-lined pathway
and the sun-blanched wooden dock,
and the unstartled man's face
which did not deign to follow
the newsprung heron in flight.

On the second night he felt
the braided rag rug bunched
beneath his feet and smoothed it
as he stepped to slide the glass
door open, its metal track
silver blue in the moonlight,
like the path and like the dock,
both smooth from his many steps
over years so he could close
his eyes and stand where he stood
at the dock's edge, Watauga
a mere step before him, low
and quiet as he opened
the fly of his sleeping pants
screenprinted with pineapples

and surfboards, a souvenir
from a homecoming event.
He took his stance, decanting,
codger on the Watauga,
and a great blue heron rose,
perhaps the same as before,
and, smiling, he gazed ahead
while the creature flew upstream.

On the third night his feet looked
silver-blue to him, the moon's
arc shifted so beams could reach
his new-woke steps to the door,
from the deck to the path, down
to the dock, all unhurried,
his body's urgency no more
than an inconvenience now,
familiar and expected.
He waited for a moment,
shifting his weight on old boards,
making an unanswered creak.
Assured that nothing had heard,
he took himself from his fly
and sniffed the faint grape odor
of his modest confluence
with the flowing Watauga.
The opposite shore lay quiet;
he heard his stream. A heron
rose without a sound and flew
upstream, unwatched but welcome.

On the fourth night, a great blue
heron glowing silver blue
in the near-full moonlight called
after flying yards away.
The conjurer turned to look
and saw a last feathered flash
and finished his long relief,
then tucked himself away, turned

as Watauga flowed in bed
to walk the silver-blue path
and mount the deck, slide the door
open, and see how past his
shadow lay his dozing wife,
silver in the near-full moon,
clear as day, her parted lips
faint whistling her sleeping breath,
the bedspread drawn and open,
not closed as he had left it,
her palm flat where he would ease
within her welcome caress.

Over Cheeseburgers at the Cottage, Thomas Crofts
and I Overhear a Valuable Lesson on Mortality
from the Raconteur, an Esteemed Former Colleague

"I tell you, fellas, it was accidental when
I stepped into the bathroom, catching her
just from the tub, as naked as a baby, pink
all over, and, you know that we've
been married nearly sixty years,
and I just fell in love again. You know
that Lovelace poem, 'Amarantha,' how
the lover wants the woman's hair kept loose,
disheveled, so perfection wouldn't be
a barrier to his approach? I stumble in,
and she just smiles, and I have hardly wished
to be a younger man again with all
that foolishness, but then, I wished
that little feller could stand up and help
me out just one last time. I would have stuck
my thumb up my rear end
and hollered 'Snake!' to scare him out."
His table laughed, and Thomas Crofts,
medievalist, and I were left to think
how great men grow; the center of
their gravity moves upward from the crotch
past gut to heart and head as years progress
and then entirely leaves the flesh.

V.

Leaving

I've dreamed this dream so many times
that I've distilled it to the car
door's opening, my standing stiff
and looking past the weathered stone
to pasture. You are grown and dressed,
like me, in heavy clothes. You wait
for me to say goodbye to those
I'll never see again; I won't
return, an older man well past
his Alabama home, and you,
who spent no more than visits here,
will think of how you'll lay my rest
much closer to the home I made for you.

Pascagoula

Pascagoula Easter Sunday
sunrise service, telling Mardi
Gras beads in my pocket, watching
sleepy, dressed-up children nestle
up against their parents, as my
small ones did, my bow-tied boys, my
ribboned girl, in patent leather
shoes with sleek, soft soles, I watch the
east for new horizon, any
hint of sun to pink the dogwood
petals. I can hear my voice in
song, "He lives! He lives!" remembered
words I cling to just outside this
prayerful circle, Easter Sunday,
Pascagoula, Mississippi.

Rolling Boil

Phyllis says she learned to roll
her kayak by resisting
the impulse to lift her head,
dipping down instead
into current, her momentum
pushing her upright again.

David runs hard, pushing
pedals, driving long trips,
never letting one bad path
spoil the journey, dripping
crawfish mud from Breaux Bridge
to his Appalachian heart
and hardly taking down time,
plotting out his next ride,
handlebar, paddle, steering wheel,
crouching down to diminish drag.

Lately I've been pausing,
waiting on submissions,
old machines and repairmen,
committees mired in days-deep
administrative inertia,
and I've been struggling
to keep my head above it,
stretching for a foothold.

When I was smaller,
a precarious step
meant nothing—a short fall—
and jumping the narrow ditch
bordering our back yard
was adventure. Those crawfish
in their little muddy holes
about broomhandle wide
weren't food fit for anyone;
even our cat wouldn't eat them.

But today, I'm bumping elbows
with other eager eaters,
pinching curled tails from bright red
creatures mud brown only
half an hour ago, before
bubbling, boiling baptism
in Zatarain fire,
unnamed bodily fluids
converted into juice, claws
into hard-to-shell treats,
thoraxes into cups
of mystery stuff too gross
to look at and too tasty
to spit out. I've witnessed
translation, eating a dare,
burning a cut on my gum
I didn't know I had,
gouging dirt and spice deep, deep
under my fingernails
and laughing about it
while our kids play and laugh
in their first round of pleasure,
their joy lacking poignancy,
nostalgia, or regret
lasting any longer
than beats between goofy jokes,
giggling distractions,
or unchecked silliness.

Bless you people. Who knew
how much I needed you
until you joined us? I vow
I will run a rough road,
risk a wrong route, retrace steps
when I get lost; when I trip,
I will resist my reflex
to brace, stiffen, or block.
I will tuck in and roll.

Molly in a Red Wig Plays a Fiddle

Molly asks me take the hanging guitar
held suspended from its two-prong hook screwed
to the wall. The guitar is her brother's,
custom-made in Vietnam, a body
brown as roux; its head and neck completely
filigreed with inlayed nacre. Hank is
working as a lawyer in Saigon. At first, I
close my eyes and let my searching fingers
find the old positions as in rhythm
I start strumming one four five. She never
names the tunes she plays, just calls them "old ones,"
Gaelic melodies through Appalachian
ache discovered by a West Coast woman
travelled more than I will ever travel.
"Do you know some Hank?" she asks me. Which ol'
Hank, I think, your brother whose guitar I'm
chording now or everybody's Hank? I
smile and nod; I wonder which of them she'll
draw, "I Saw the Light," "Your Cheatin' Heart"? No,
neither one will fit tonight. She settles
on a plaintive "I'm So Lonesome, I Could
Cry," and I am watching Molly's bow; she
never counts, her timing shifts for feeling,
she keeps playing 'til imagined dancers
drop, and neither of us knows the lyrics
front to back; they're just familiar lonesome
lines the other guests forgot the words to,
first duet, too blue, October evening.

Mulberries

I hiked a loved trail made of tarmack macadam crust and peered through
    undergrowth cove shade of converted abandoned locomotive track,
    taken in, a stranger covered by green tint veiled leaf light.
Melissa Helton sat by me at the mulberry-stained iron chairs,
    companion; we heard the whisper of the creek, clear and without
    secrets, ankle-deep by the coffeehouse seeming made for empathy,
the rounded pebbles on the creekbed smooth as the ball of my writing
    hand, my ring and little finger curled to press that fleshy cushion as I
    fidgeted to fill lines, discontent in this comfort.
Look at the mulberries, she said, the branches overhanging Gap Creek
    as full of berries as the berries were themselves of purple burst, ready
    for creatures wary of the patrons.
What is this protocol of fruit and berry trees that no one harvests, food
    as ornament,
where once the campus where I work was covered with persimmon and
    crabapple, sharp, tart, but filling, so peripatetic professors, snatching
    bites, could invite the underclassmen to feed and learn,
where, these past three years, I saw the matronly Latina rescue the near-
    windfall peaches from the thwarted tree trapped in a grass strip
    between a Papa John's and the street,
where, in the wet overplenty, I could invite the neighbor children to take
    what they could reach before the apple tree's full branches with their
    overburden broke,
not a violation of an orchard or the theft from a roadside garden, I know
    so many who give freely of that plenty, glad to share,
but that fruit which dangles freely on a branch above some shallow
    water, windwhipped slightly out of reach?
I thought I could taste them, sitting, gazing, dozing in shifting sunlight
and heard Melissa chuckle as she shook her sandals off
and placed her chair down in the shallows, shifting pebbles, spurting
    four brief plumes of sediment that drifted quick and settled yards
    downstream,
and stood as steady on the wrought-iron seat as if it were a stair; she
    filled a cup to brimming, eating berries while she picked and picked,
    her fingers pinching stems, except a single berry, slipping, bouncing
    from chair-arm lattice to the crystal water that had come from
    deep within the woods, that drizzled, dripped, or fell itself, before,
    then sought itself and joined and surfaced, traced a bellied bed

and streamed, inviting growth and succor, fresh relief from silence,
  stillness, dryness, bitter dark,
the berry, rolling in the listless current, resting as it lodged against a gray
  slate cleft.
I loosed my heavy boots and rolled my thick socks to my toes; I dropped
  my socks inside my boots; I waded to the slate and fished the berry
  from its notch.
What caution? Tenderfoot and trailspent, still, retrieving just one bite
  was sunlight, beaming down, reflecting up, and sweet,
I felt I'd found some words I hadn't found.
Melissa laughed, climbed down, and offered me her cup,
and I could not accept it, and I could not voice "thank you," although she
  saw how, grateful, slowly I climbed up the bank
and stuffed my wet but now-socked feet into my "sta-dri" boots.
A gift is not a thing but love, communion of shared affinity, like song
  catching some within hearing who cannot help but mouth the
  words, like voicedrawn infants who reflect in their expressions those
  who speak to them until, at last, they huff and stop their breaths to
  what inflection they might master, flat or round, atonal or musical,
  slightly off key and out of time like unfamiliar intimacy unfelt until
  immersed.

Old 31

The Hives

On 31, the old one headed north
through Cullman County, almost to West Point,
my father's parents lived, cement block house
within a short ten yards of faded stripe
just barely yellow two-lane road, a ditch
this side, the other side a pasture fenced
with barbed wire nailed to wooden posts.
Behind the house, a meager stream, a rise
up to the fields close bordered by the hives
he kept for years, white painted hives of bees
whose hum would fill the afternoon in spring
as I would go between the house and rise
to feel the shade from high white oaks and play
in slow stream water, count the fish
that darted rock to rock, surprise a frog
or maybe rouse a turtle brown as stone.
I pushed his old reel mower, handle grey
as wood can get exposed to elements
yet smooth from handling over years of use,
the blades whirr whispering and lopping heads
from standing clover, scarcely loud enough
to mask the trickling water wash nearby
where moss was soft beneath bare feet new wet
from wading, toeing stone aside to press
brown sediment and watch it wash away
between my toes as light as smoke that rose
that far in spring from burning off the stalks
from last year's corn. I was a boy back then.

Carport

My father built the carport cover low
enough where I could reach its frame. He'd dug
four postholes, plumbed the posts, and mixed Quikrete.
He tamped the earth himself. He hung its frame,
its latching pans of corrugated white
aluminum, a heavy gauge held fast

in place with large self-tapping screws. He pulled
his father's Galaxie beneath, its red
taillights like booster rockets braked to burn.

Kitchen

I must have eaten there when I was small,
but I cannot recall; we visited
midafternoons and left before the time
to cook. He sent commodities with us,
great blocks of yellow cheese, big cans of meat
in round and oily chunks, and sacks of beans.
Their cabinets were simple, white, and cool.
A corrugated metal draining board
beside the sink let drops of water bead,
connect, and drip into the suds. The chairs
were metal tubing, vinyl cushions, cold
just like Formica on the table, cold.
She had a plastic radio. I changed
the station once but never did again.

Larder

The northeast corner off the kitchen, cool
and shadowy in summer, lined with shelves
and cabinets, their larder lured me days
when thirsty gulps of sulfurous water weren't
enough to soothe me from humidity
and heat. I loved the dark and dry, the sound
of nothing cushioned, barefoot sticky slaps
on painted concrete floor, the jars of fruit,
of beans, of peeled tomatoes, lined on shelves
as regular as prayer, combs of gold-
spun honey catching what spare light would fall
down, filter through thick white oak foliage,
its single table, single chair a place
a boy could sit and trace with fingertips
the woodgrain varnished brown as new-tilled earth.

Den

They huddled on a sofa side by side,
a shoebox full of photos in her lap,
and she, her voice long lost to stroke,
would take a photo, hand it over, elbow him
until he guessed the gossip she would share
if she could speak, her scowl as permanent
as tissue wads in her left hand that caught
the drool from her turned lip. He petted her
and called her "Sally," patient and in love.
This tiny room, a butane heater hulked
so close to them they seemed to shrink, held six
of us until we boys would wander off—
the bedrooms were forbidden to us both—
outside to get away was best, but, stuck,
I'd browse through months-old papers full of ads,
Progressive Farmer magazines, and, once,
somebody's schoolbook left behind that had
a poem in it where a father has
his ailing child on horseback, and the child
can see a threat the worried man cannot.

Living Room

A closed-off winter room where I would go
to leave the roasting den, the living room
in summer was the route to their front porch.
Thick curtains closed the musty furniture
so showroom stiff I didn't want to sit
and watch faint tv signals lulled between
the nearest markets drawn by rabbit ears
to coalescing static, tv snow.
To stay until my knuckles ached, my breath
a trace above me, there I rocked and watched
the changing image hung by the front door,
the Christ lenticular, whose brow,
untroubled, glowed in golden rays, to shift
and see Him stand beside a door to knock

in hopes of welcome when in winter they
expected folks to go around the back.

Because Cucumbers

Garden grove walls
because not the sterile mint of a hospital waiting room, the dusky
    Lincoln of a legendary archer, the utilitarian deep spring of a tractor,
because the ivy clinging to the walls of the first house my wife and I
    bought together, where we have raised our children,
because the vinyl landau roof of the car we drove in our young married
    move out of state,
because the shirt I wore the day I took my oldest off to college,
because the inherited family hunger for color on interior walls protected
    by the sun-bleached clapboard outside,
because the magnolia leaves of the tree I took seed pods from, tying
    them with twine and pitching them around the powerlines outside
    the house of an old man who loved me,
because cucumbers,
because her chalkboard, on which the first woman I ever loved outside
    my family taught me letters and numbers, symbols and punctuation,
because the new moss encircling the roots of the great oak outside my
    childhood bedroom window,
because the biker bar in Neptune Beach, Jacksonville, Florida,
because the fantasy of dropping from my seat until only my eyes peer
    above my desk, like a gator just submerged, as someone enters my
    office,
because the tresses of algae in the creek half an acre from my
    grandfather's beehives, where my brother would run as that good
    man would rob them.

Notes

Page 22: In "Trencher," the word "cyarn" should be pronounced as if the "c" were a /k/, as in "carnage." I would hear the word "cyarn" applied to types of nastiness associated with decay, not necessarily of only flesh.

Page 40: "Covenant" refers to Zipporah's performing a circumcision on her infant son and smearing some of the blood on Moses to avert God's wrath. The account from the King James Version of Exodus 4:24-26 is as follows:

> [24] And it came to pass by the way in the inn, that the Lord met him, and sought to kill him.
> [25] Then Zipporah took a sharp stone, and cut off the foreskin of her son, and cast it at his feet, and said, Surely a bloody husband art thou to me.
> [26] So he let him go: then she said, A bloody husband thou art, because of the circumcision.

The repetition of "he" without clear referents makes different interpretations possible.

Page 67: "Haruspication" involves reading entrails to determine the future.

Page 84: "Old 31" alludes to "Erlkönig," by Johann Wolfgang von Goethe.

A native Alabamian, Thomas Alan Holmes spent many years on the staff and masthead of *The Black Warrior Review* while completing his graduate degrees at the University of Alabama. He is co-editor of *Walking the Line: Country Music Lyricists and American Culture* (with Roxanne Harde, Lexington Books, 2013), *Jeff Daniel Marion: Poet on the Holston* (with Jesse Graves and Ernest Lee, University of Tennessee Press, 2015), and *The Fire That Breaks: Gerard Manley Hopkins's Poetic Legacies* (with Daniel Westover, Clemson University Press, 2020). His research and creative work have appeared in such journals as *Louisiana Review*, *Valparaiso Poetry Review*, *The Connecticut Review*, *Appalachian Heritage*, *Blue Mesa Review*, *Still: The Journal*, and *Appalachian Journal*. He and his family live in Johnson City, Tennessee, where he specializes in Appalachian and African American literature as a professor of English at East Tennessee State University.

CPSIA information can be obtained
at www.ICGtesting.com
Printed in the USA
BVHW042351230722
642879BV00001B/96